TANKS

by Jeffrey Zuehlke

Lerner Publications Company • Minneapolis

For the troops

Text copyright © 2006 by Lerner Publications Company

Lerner Publications Company
A division of Lerner Publishing Group
241 First Avenue North
Minneapolis, MN 55401 U.S.A.

Website address: www.lernerbooks.com

Library of Congress Cataloging-in-Publication Data

Zuehlke, Jeffrey, 1968–
    Tanks / by Jeffrey Zuehlke.
      p.   cm. – (Pull ahead books)
    Includes index.
    ISBN-13: 978-0-8225-2865-4 (lib. bdg. : alk. paper)
    ISBN-10: 0-8225-2865-7 (lib. bdg. : alk. paper)
    1. Tanks (Military science)—Juvenile literature. I. Title.
  II. Series.
  UG446.5.Z84 2006
  623.7'4752–dc22   2005005654

Manufactured in the United States of America
1 2 3 4 5 6 – JR – 11 10 09 08 07 06

Rumble, rumble, rumble. What's that coming this way?

It's a tank! Tanks are fighting machines.
They have powerful weapons.

Tanks also have thick **armor**. It protects them from bullets and bombs.

Hey! What's on those wheels?
Tank wheels have tracks.

The wheels turn. They move the tracks.
The tracks grip the ground. They move
the tank.

Tanks can drive just about anywhere.
Tanks can drive through dirt and sand.

They can drive over bushes and fences.

Some tanks can even drive
through water!

This is an M1 Abrams tank. The M1 is the toughest tank in the world.

Stingrays are light tanks. They are small and fast.

Bradley Fighting Vehicles are fast and powerful. They carry people to battle.

Who uses tanks?
Soldiers do.
They use tanks
for fighting.

This is the tank's **crew**. Each person has a special job.

The driver
steers the
tank.

The driver sits in the front of the **hull**.
The hull is the main part of the tank.

The **commander** is in charge of the
tank. The commander tells the driver
where to go.

The commander sits in the **turret**.
The turret turns all the way around.

The turret has a **cannon**. When the turret turns, the cannon turns with it.

Boom! That's a big gun!

The **loader** loads the cannon.

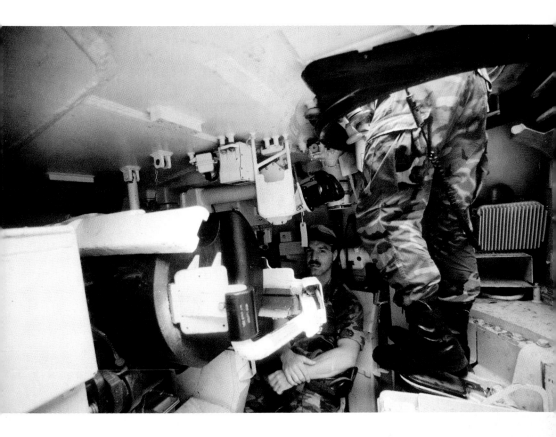

The **gunner** aims and fires the cannon.
The gunner uses a computer to help
find the target.

The crew climbs through **hatches** to get in and out of the tank. The hatches can be shut tight.

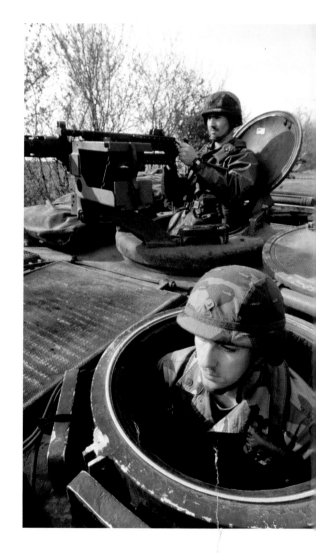

Tanks don't just fight. They carry stuff too.

This tank is carrying a bridge.
It can set the bridge down over
a river or a ditch.

Soldiers can use the bridge to cross
the ditch. The tank has saved the day!
Say thanks to the tank!

Facts about Tanks

■ The U.S. Army and the U.S. Marine Corps use tanks for fighting.

■ The first tanks were used in 1916 during World War I.

■ In 2005, U.S. tanks helped troops to do their jobs in Iraq and Afghanistan.

■ Different types of U.S. tanks are named after famous military leaders. Tanks have names like Abrams, Sherman, Patton, and Sheridan.

■ The U.S. Army's M1 Abrams tank is one of the most powerful tanks in the world. It has some of the best weapons and strongest armor.

Parts of a Tank

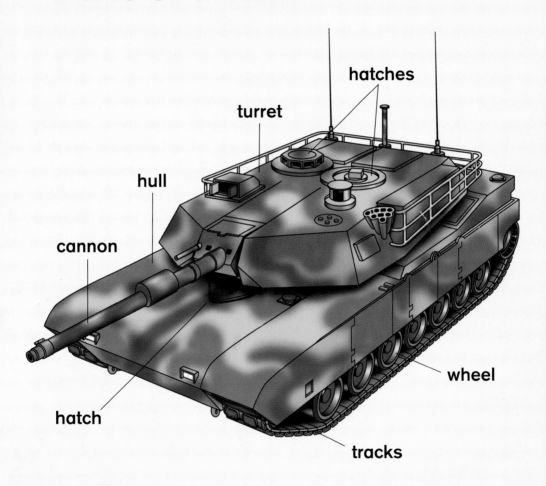

hatches

turret

hull

cannon

hatch

wheel

tracks

29

Glossary

armor: thick material that protects the tank from bullets and bombs

cannon: a big gun

commander: the person in charge of a tank

crew: the people who work in a tank

gunner: the person who aims and fires the cannon

hatches: openings that can be shut tight

hull: the main part of a tank

loader: the person who loads the cannon

turret: the top part of a tank that turns all the way around

Index

About the Author

Jeffrey Zuehlke has never ridden in a tank, but he has seen them up close. He's even knocked on their tough armor and poked his head inside. Jeffrey likes to read books about tanks and military history while sitting in a comfortable chair at his home in Minneapolis, Minnesota.

Photo Acknowledgments

The photographs in this book appear courtesy of: Staff Sgt. Shane A. Cuomo/U.S. Air Force/United States Department of Defense, cover; © General Dynamics Land Systems, pp. 3, 4, 5, 7, 8, 11,14, 20, 21, 25, 26, 27, 31; Cpl. Mike Vrabel/U.S. Marines, p. 6; Sgt. Oscar Martinez, U.S. Marine Corps/United States Department of Defense, p. 9; U.S. Marines, p. 10; © Textron Marine & Land Systems, p. 12; Senior Airman Jeffrey Allen, U.S. Air Force/United States Department of Defense, p. 13; Lance Cpl. G. Lane Miley/U.S. Marines, p. 15; © Wernher Krutein/Photovault.com, pp. 16, 23; Defense Visual Information Center, p. 17; © Leif Skoogfors/CORBIS, pp. 18, 24; Cpl Rick O'Connor/U.S. Marines, p. 19; Gunnery Sgt. Rob Blakenship/U.S. Marines, p. 22.